The Amazing POTATO Book

Written by
Paulette Bourgeois

with the National Museum of
Science and Technology

Illustrated by
Linda Hendry

▲▲ **Addison-Wesley Publishing Company, Inc.**
Reading, Massachusetts   Menlo Park, California   New York
Don Mills, Ontario   Wokingham, England   Amsterdam   Bonn
Sydney   Singapore   Tokyo   Madrid   San Juan
Paris   Seoul   Milan   Mexico City   Taipei

Acknowledgements

This book was made possible because of the knowledgeable, helpful and generous support of the staff of the National Museum of Science and Technology in Ottawa, Ontario, Canada. They gave me access to all the research material for their Amazing Potato exhibit and spent hours showing me artifacts and explaining details. I am especially grateful to Wendy McPeake, Chief of Publications; Tom Brown, Curator of Agricultural Technology; George Nicholson, assistant curator; researcher Mireille Macia; Victoria Dickenson for supplementary research; Maggie Dorning, Colette Morin and the others who shared their time, information and insights.

My gratitude extends to Beth Evans who researched tricky statistical and scientific queries, Hostess, Humpty Dumpty, McCain's, Patricia Manning of the Prince Edward Island Department of Agriculture Marketing Services, E.C. Lougheed of the University of Guelph, Nancy G. Dengler of the University of Toronto, the Royal Ontario Museum, the ever-helpful librarians of Boys and Girls House and the North York Central Library.

And, as usual, I thank all the terrific people at Kids Can Press who make amazing books happen, with a special note of appreciation to Liz MacLeod and Ronda Arab.

**Library of Congress
Cataloging-in-Publication Data**

Bourgeois, Paulette.
 The amazing potato book / written by
Paulette Bourgeois ; illustrated by Linda Hendry.
  p. cm.
 Includes index.
 Summary: Examines the history, cultivation, uses, and other aspects of the amazing potato.
 ISBN 0-201-56761-X
 1. Potatoes–Juvenile literature.
 2. Potatoes–Utilization–Juvenile literature.
 [1. Potatoes.] I. Hendry, Linda, ill. II. Title.
SB211.P8B76   1991
635′.21–dc20   91-23847
                                                         CIP
                                                         AC

Edited by Elizabeth MacLeod
Designed by Michael Solomon
Set in 12-point Primer by Techni Process Lettering Ltd.

Contents

*I*f what you already know about potatoes can be summed up in just three words — mashed, fried, and baked — then this is the book for you. Did you know that potatoes owe their popularity to greedy gold-diggers and wars? And how about the idea that potato chips might never have been invented if it weren't for an unhappy customer at the Moon Lake Lodge? Did you know that potatoes can be deadly? Eating potatoes or parts of the leafy potato plant can make you very, very queasy or even kill you. (Blame it on a skeleton in the potato family closet.) Read on and discover more about these amazing spud facts.

Discover how an angry chef made an earth-shattering, mouth-watering discovery by slicing his french fries too thin, in Chapter 1, starting on page 6.

Find out how the Spanish conquistadores almost died in their search for a lost city of gold in the Amazon jungles until they discovered the Inca's secret for survival — the potato. See Chapter 2, starting on page 16.

Stranded on a desert island? Don't worry, as long as you have a sack of potatoes — 23 potatoes a day keep the doctors away. And, as a bonus, you'll be able to say, "Look, Pa. No cavities!" when the rescue ship comes by. There's more about what's in a potato and why it's important in Chapter 3, starting on page 36.

Want to know why green potatoes can make you sick and why parts of the plant can be deadly? Read about Killer Potatoes in Chapter 4, starting on page 46.

After those deadly facts, you might want to lighten up with a potato picnic and throw a few hot potatoes around! The fun starts in Chapter 5, on page 58.

Find out the true story of Mr. Potato Head, make a potato print, whip up a chocolate-potato dessert that will have your guests begging for more, and find out how potatoes may save the world's poor children from hunger.

All of this plus games, experiments, jokes, puzzles, fun activities and more in **The Amazing Potato Book.**

If you find a potato word that you don't understand, check the glossary at the back of the book for an explanation.

1.
Potatoes:
a positively perfect passion

Get into your time machine and set the clock for 1929.
Ready? Whew! Check out those clothes you're wearing!
Now, head into the kitchen and open the cupboards
to grab a snack.

How about some dried apples? Not in the mood? All right, how about some of those home-made cookies? They look terrific, but you had something else in mind. Something that goes crunch and fills your whole mouth. Something with a lingering bit of oil and salt to satisfy those late afternoon cravings. That's it – a bag of potato chips. But you'll have to turn your time-machine dial to the time of the Second World War before you'll find factory-made potato chips in a bag!

Today, potato chips are the biggest selling snack food in the United States and Canada. If you lined up 100 people eating snacks, 70 of them would be munching on potato chips. Some people eat more and some people eat less, but on average, every person eats 3 kg (6½ lbs) of potato chips a year. That's nine family size chip bags EACH!

Nobody can eat just one

The first potato chip

It's hard to imagine that nobody had invented potato chips until almost 150 years ago. We know that the pioneers didn't make potato chips. Like so many other inventions, the potato chip came about by accident. A chef named George Crum was working at a very ritzy resort called the Moon Lake Lodge in Saratoga Springs, New York. He was proud of his thick french-fried potatoes. But one guest didn't agree: he said the fried potatoes were too thick and sent them back to the kitchen.

The chef was insulted. He cut the chips thinner and fried them again. The guest *still* didn't like them and sent them back. By this time, Chef Crum was furious. "Hmmmm," he thought, "I'll show the customers never to complain about my potatoes!" He sliced the potatoes so thin that he could see through them and then he tossed them into hot oil. To his surprise, the fussy customer loved the potato chips. They were passed around the table and everybody loved them. The chef called his invention Saratoga Chips and made them the house specialty!

At first, the chips were served as a side dish, as if they were mashed or baked potatoes. It was hard work making potato chips because they had to be peeled and sliced by hand. Then in 1920, some bright person invented the potato-peeling machine and soon factories producing potato chips opened. However, only Easterners who lived on the coast or along the Canada-U.S.A. border had potato chips all the time.

A travelling salesman from Tennessee changed all that. In 1932 Herman Lay filled the trunk of his Model A Ford with bags of potato chips and started selling them to store owners across the southern United States. Lay's potato chips became the first national brand of North America's favourite crispy, crunchy snack.

In 1958, the H.W. Lay Company introduced another type of chip named Ruffles. Ruffles have ridges because the blades that slice the potatoes are rippled instead of straight. Today Lay's and Ruffles chips use about 8% of all the potatoes grown in the United States.

How potato chips are made

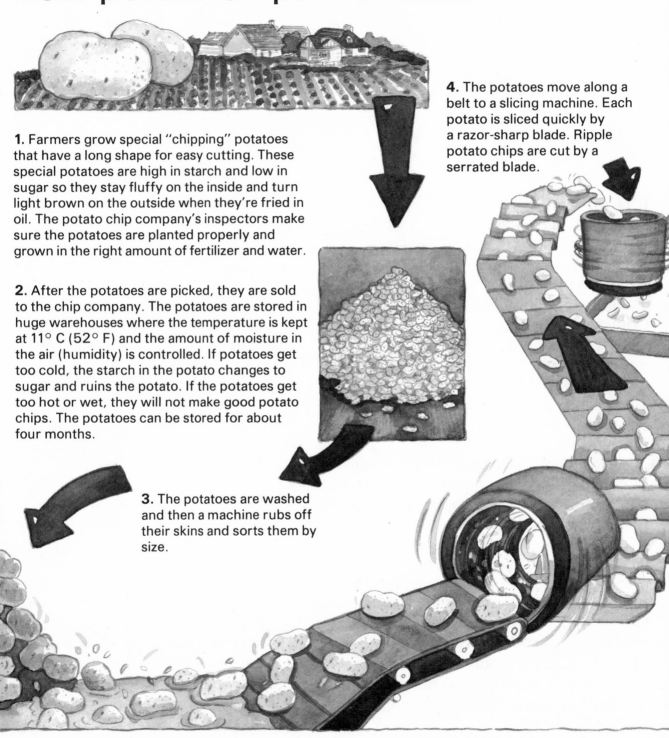

1. Farmers grow special "chipping" potatoes that have a long shape for easy cutting. These special potatoes are high in starch and low in sugar so they stay fluffy on the inside and turn light brown on the outside when they're fried in oil. The potato chip company's inspectors make sure the potatoes are planted properly and grown in the right amount of fertilizer and water.

2. After the potatoes are picked, they are sold to the chip company. The potatoes are stored in huge warehouses where the temperature is kept at 11° C (52° F) and the amount of moisture in the air (humidity) is controlled. If potatoes get too cold, the starch in the potato changes to sugar and ruins the potato. If the potatoes get too hot or wet, they will not make good potato chips. The potatoes can be stored for about four months.

3. The potatoes are washed and then a machine rubs off their skins and sorts them by size.

4. The potatoes move along a belt to a slicing machine. Each potato is sliced quickly by a razor-sharp blade. Ripple potato chips are cut by a serrated blade.

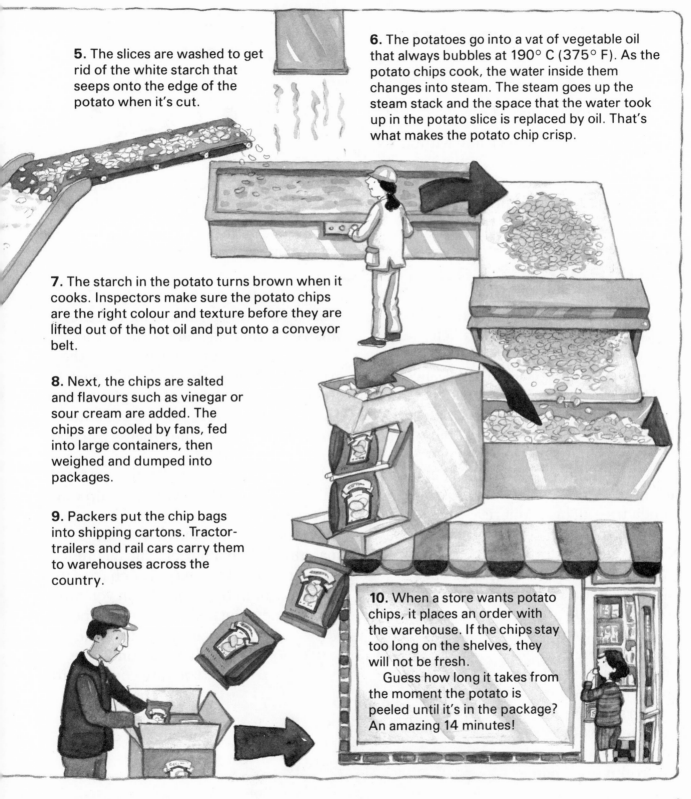

5. The slices are washed to get rid of the white starch that seeps onto the edge of the potato when it's cut.

6. The potatoes go into a vat of vegetable oil that always bubbles at 190° C (375° F). As the potato chips cook, the water inside them changes into steam. The steam goes up the steam stack and the space that the water took up in the potato slice is replaced by oil. That's what makes the potato chip crisp.

7. The starch in the potato turns brown when it cooks. Inspectors make sure the potato chips are the right colour and texture before they are lifted out of the hot oil and put onto a conveyor belt.

8. Next, the chips are salted and flavours such as vinegar or sour cream are added. The chips are cooled by fans, fed into large containers, then weighed and dumped into packages.

9. Packers put the chip bags into shipping cartons. Tractor-trailers and rail cars carry them to warehouses across the country.

10. When a store wants potato chips, it places an order with the warehouse. If the chips stay too long on the shelves, they will not be fresh.

Guess how long it takes from the moment the potato is peeled until it's in the package? An amazing 14 minutes!

Check out your chip I.Q.

Take this true or false quiz about potato chips.

(Answers on page 64.)

1. Potato chips can be made without potatoes.
2. Potato chips are a protein food.
3. There's lots of vitamin C in potato chips.

4. You could survive on potato chips.
5. Potato chips are loaded with salt and fat.

Some like them fried

Potato chips aren't the only snack food that potato fanatics crave. French fries have been around since 1700 when cooks in France cut potatoes into thick slices and fried them. The American ambassador to France at the time, Thomas Jefferson, liked the french fries so much that when he later became president and moved into the White House, he asked his chef to make them. Soon, you could find thick-cut french fries all over America.

Now french fries win the grand prize as North America's favourite food. We eat a total of 12 BILLION kilograms (26 BILLION pounds) of them each year. If you made a pile of all those fries, it would weigh more than 33,500 Boeing 747 jumbo jets stacked one on top of the other.

At first, all french fries were made fresh, but today more people eat frozen fries than fresh fries. Bet you already know the answer to this question: What is the biggest-selling frozen vegetable in the world? Of course, frozen french fries. At the largest frozen french-fry plant in the United States, the factory never shuts down and 1,500 people process 100,000 potatoes each hour!

People don't have to dig in their freezer, go to a restaurant or even to a chip wagon on the street to get a "fry fix." A Canadian inventor has made the first vending machine for french fries. The machine contains slightly cooked french fries in a refrigerator in the back. When you put in your money, the potatoes are dumped into bubbling hot oil. In 90 seconds the fries are cooked, lifted out of the hot oil and poured into a cardboard container!

Make french fries

People around the world have favourite ways of eating their french fries. Did you know that in Holland people eat their fries with mayonnaise, while in the United States, most people like ketchup on their fries? In Canada, people prefer their fries with white vinegar, and in Quebec, there's a french-fry fad called "poutine." That's french fries with gravy and cheese curds.

Most french fries are cooked in oil. But hot oil is dangerous since it can splatter and burn the cook, or start a fire. Besides, a lot of fat isn't good for you. Instead, make these oven fries the next time you're craving a fry fix!

You'll need:

4 large baking potatoes
a kitchen knife
15 mL (1 tbsp) vegetable oil
a small bowl
a large non-stick cookie sheet
oven mitts
a metal spatula

1. Preheat the oven to 245° C (475° F).
2. Wash and scrub the potatoes. Do not peel. Cut the potatoes lengthwise into 1 cm (½ inch) thick slices. Cut each of those slices into .5 cm (¼ inch) strips.

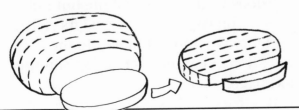

3. Pour the oil into the bowl. In small batches, toss the french fries in the oil then put them on the cookie sheet.

4. Bake for 25 minutes.
5. Wearing your oven mitts, take the cookie sheets out of the oven and flip the fries with the spatula.

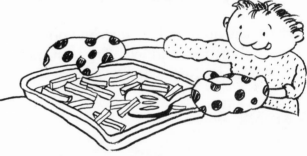

6. Bake for another 10 minutes. Sprinkle with a little salt or parmesan cheese and enjoy.
Serves 4.

What do you call a baby potato?

A small fry.

It's fun to be able to do something that nobody else can do. Usually, there's some kind of trick involved. Here are two challenges that are bound to amaze your friends.

Make a potato wobble

Even if you have the I.Q. of a genius, you'll enjoy this wobbly potato. Just in case you think the activity is mindless, try to figure out why it wobbles and doesn't fall over!

You'll need:

4 matchsticks
2 potatoes
wire cutters
a wire coat hanger

1. Stick the matchsticks into one potato to resemble arms and legs. Try to stand the potato up. Impossible?

2. Cut the coat hanger so that you have a piece of wire 12 cm (5 inches) long. Bend it so that it looks like the wire below.

3. Stick one end of the coat hanger piece into the "belly" of your potato person.
4. Stick the other end of the coat hanger piece into the other potato.

5. Put your potato person on the edge of a shelf so that the whole potato hangs over the edge.

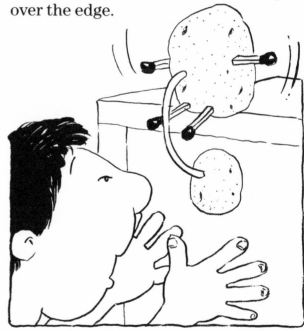

6. Watch it wobble.

Why does your potato wobble but not topple? You've just discovered its centre of gravity. To find out more, do the "question of balance" challenge on the next page.

A question of balance

Ask your friends to balance a slice of potato on the end of a pencil. Chances are they'll be stumped. Here's how to do it.

You'll need:
   a sewing needle
   half a potato
   2 forks
   a pencil with flat eraser end

1. Push the needle into the centre of the narrowest end of the potato so that the needle sticks out less than 2.5 cm (1 inch).

2. Stick a fork into each side of the potato half so that the handles hang down. Try sticking the forks about half-way down the potato.

3. Hold the pencil in one hand. Put the point of the needle on the eraser. It should balance. If it doesn't, try moving the forks so that they hang closer to the pencil.

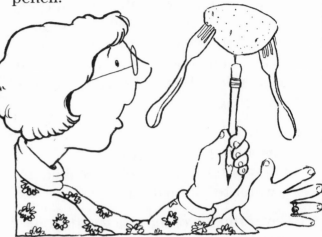

4. Once the potato is balanced, try to give it a spin. What happens?

Congratulate yourself. You've just done a physics experiment in equilibrium (balance) and gravity.

If you try to balance a piece of potato on the point of a needle you can't do it. That's because with all the potato's lumps and bumps, you can't place the needle exactly underneath the potato's centre of gravity, also called the balancing point. When you stab the forks into the potato, the weight of the forks moves the centre of gravity. If you place the forks just right, the potato's balancing point moves so that it's right on top of the needle.

The minute your "potato-needle-fork-pencil-thing" stays still, you've discovered the balancing point.

A thick skin

You can astound your friends by saying you can plunge a flimsy straw through the middle of a raw potato. Most of them will say the task is impossible. Others will claim it's easy, try it and wind up with a bunch of bent straws. They'll bet you can't do it. Here's the trick to prove them wrong.

You'll need:
   a paper or plastic straw
   a new potato, or old potato soaked in
      water to soften its skin

1. Cover the top of the straw with your thumb.
2. Plunge the straw as hard as you can

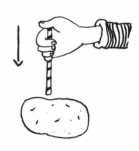

into the middle of the potato. Make sure that you hold the straw perfectly straight so that it is perpendicular to the surface of the potato.

When you put your thumb over the top of the straw, you stop air from escaping. Then, when you apply force (when you push down suddenly) and hit the potato, the air inside the straw is under pressure. The thin skin of a new potato or the soft skin of a water-logged potato is no match for a straw full of compressed air.

Stain-removing power!

Spilled some ketchup on your clothes and don't have any stain remover? Don't worry. Rub a potato over the stain and — abracadabra! The stain starts to disappear. You can experiment without actually spilling on your clothes.

You'll need:
   a piece of old clothing or scrap
      material
   a spoonful of ketchup
   a spoonful of mustard
   a spoonful of oil
   half a potato
   laundry soap
   water

1. Put your material on a washable surface, such as a counter or table.
2. Rub in some of each of the staining ingredients. Try dirt, grape juice or other "tough dirties" too.
3. Let the stains dry.
4. Rub the potato vigorously over the stain.

5. Wash the fabric with soap and water.
6. Did your environmentally-safe stain remover work?

Potatoes beyond the table

Sure you know that potatoes are wonderful to eat, but do you realize that potatoes could fuel your car, keep athletes comfortable, and make ice cream thicker and smoother?

When Henry Ford started making automobiles at the beginning of this century, he worried that the world would run out of cheap gas for his cars. Instead of digging oil wells, Ford imported potatoes from Europe and started a massive potato field. He knew that when potatoes are mashed and left in the air, they ferment and make ethyl alcohol. Ford had a vision of cars getting around on "potato gasohol"! But since there was no energy shortage in Henry's day, and lots of petroleum gas around, the fields were abandoned. Too bad, because his idea was a good one. Scientists have discovered that less than .5 hectare (1 acre) of potatoes can produce enough gas to fill up 25 station wagons.

But how do athletes benefit from potatoes? Silky soft powders to stop tight shoes or athletic equipment from rubbing can be made from potato starch. Ahhhhh! Relief! Even make-up is made with potato starch.

And in Idaho Falls, Idaho, Reed's Dairy proudly adds potato flakes to make smooth, creamy ice cream. They even advertise on their container that Reed's ice cream is "Made with Idaho Potatoes!"

Actually, potatoes are hidden in many things that you enjoy eating. Potatoes are added to soups, sauces, pasta, baked goods and low-fat dairy products to help the foods stick together, stop ice crystals from forming in frozen foods or to make food creamier.

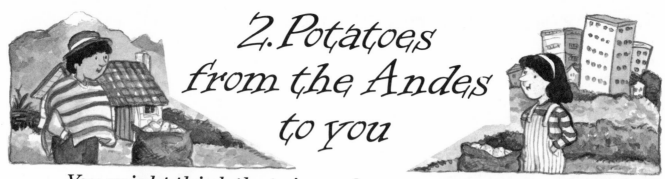

2. Potatoes from the Andes to you

You might think that since almost every man, woman and child from coast to coast eats some kind of potato each day, potatoes have been part of the North American diet since the beginning of time. It's a logical assumption, but a wrong one.

Potatoes don't grow wild in most parts of the United States and Canada. It took some inventive South American Indians and some greedy and hungry European explorers to make North America meat-and-potatoes country. Follow the potato path from the Andes to North America and discover how potatoes made a journey around the world to become the most popular vegetable on the globe.

Life and death in the Andes

Ten thousand years ago the ice age was just coming to an end in North America. But in South America, natives were growing crops in the steamy jungles of the Amazon Basin. They could have lived there happily forever except that fierce, marauding tribes forced the local Indians up the Andes mountains in search of peace and safety. By 2500 BC, the Indians were living on a barren, frigid Andean plateau 3 km (2 miles) high in the sky. It was a harsh existence. Blizzards blew even in August and there could be killing frost in the middle of summer.

But the Indians survived because they

learned how to grow and store the pebble-sized purple, red and yellow vegetables that grew underground. They called them *papas* (PAW-pus). Later, in other countries, these vegetables would be known as potatoes. The tiny rugged plants survived even when the leaves withered on frosty nights. Since it was the only thing to eat, the Indians learned how to cultivate and use the *papas* all year long. They didn't know it, but their *papas* were rich in almost all the nutrients the Indians needed to survive.

The growing, gathering and storing of *papas* was an almost full-time village activity. It took three people to dig out all the tiny potatoes: two to lever the potatoes out of the ground with a tool called a *taclla* (TACK-lee-a) and another to lift away the earth and uncover the *papas*. The natives couldn't work long in the thin air before they collapsed in exhaustion.

(Even today when tourists visit a hotel on the Andean plateau, they are warned not to close their windows tightly on cold nights. There is so little oxygen in the air at those altitudes that an unsuspecting tourist might breathe up all the oxygen in the room and die fighting for air.)

Ancient instant potatoes

The Indians grew two kinds of potato crops. The first was called *chchoqhe* (CHOE-kay) and it was similar to a baking potato. The Indians baked it in hot coals, just as you would roast potatoes at a campfire.

The second type of crop, the *lukki* (LOU-key) potatoes, could grow in almost any weather, but the flesh was bitter when baked. The Indians turned those potatoes into a dried food called *chuño* (CHOON-yo) that could be eaten throughout the winter. Here's how they made it: once the *lukki* potatoes were harvested, they were placed under a bed of straw and left outside. For nights on end, the potatoes froze. When the *lukkis* were shrivelled and watery, the workers laid another layer of straw on top. Then the entire village stomped on the potatoes! When all the water was squished out, the potatoes were left in the sun to dry.

The potatoes could be stored in a dry place over winter. For dinner, the Indians mixed the *chuño* with water and other vegetables and cooked the mixture into a stew. But it wasn't an international gourmet hit. When the explorers came, they wrote home to say that they had eaten the native food and that it not only looked like cork, it tasted like it too!

The potato spirit

Since potatoes were so essential to the South American Indians, it's no surprise that they were worshipped and thought of as possessing supernatural powers. When the Incas ruled Peru, the ruler would call the local fortune teller to his home. She would be asked to count a heap of potatoes in pairs. If there was a potato left over, the year ahead was supposed to be unlucky.

Many centuries later, in 400 AD, the Chimu people of Peru made human sacrifices to the spirit who guarded the potato crops. Archeologists think that the Chimu mutilated their victims to make them look more like the potatoes in the region. These potatoes have very deep eyes, so deep that they look like gaping mouths with teeth. The Indians had discovered that the potatoes with the largest "mouths" could be cut up to grow the most potatoes the next season. What better way to please the spirit than to cut large mouths into their sacrifice?

The conquistadores ate potatoes

Potatoes might never have left South America if the Spaniards hadn't gone searching for gold to mine and for a legendary, hidden city made entirely of gold called El Dorado.

These gold-greedy explorers, the conquistadores, forced the Incas to be their slaves in the gold and silver mines. And while the conquistadores got rich from the mines, they kept searching for El Dorado. They slogged through the steamiest jungles, trudged through the murkiest piranha-rich rivers and scaled mountains. They almost died of sickness and starvation. By the time they got to the cold upper plateau of the Andes mountains, they were freezing and starving, and their teeth were falling out. They survived because the Indians introduced them to *papas*.

Grow an unpotato

Guess what plant is the potato's closest relative. Did you guess a sweet potato? Nope. You'll probably never guess. It's an eggplant. Sweet potatoes are not even related to the potato. Potatoes belong to the nightshade family and sweet potatoes belong to the trailing vine family. Still, all the plants look alike, and cooks say that you can make the same recipes with a potato or a sweet potato.

Centuries ago when European sailors brought home from the West Indies a new vegetable, an oval-shaped, sweet, orange root, they called it by its native name, *batatas*. The people in Europe soon discovered that the *batatas* was sugary and made it into a delicious home-made candy.

Sweet potatoes still taste great cooked and mashed with spices such as cinnamon and orange juice. And sweet potatoes are a cinch to grow. After a short time of observing your plant, you'll see how close a cousin the sweet potato is to a beautiful flowering vine called the morning glory plant.

You'll need:
- 3 toothpicks
- a sweet potato – an organic one is best because you know it hasn't been treated with a chemical that prevents growing.
- a jar or container with a narrow opening
- water

1. Stick the toothpicks around the centre of the sweet potato.

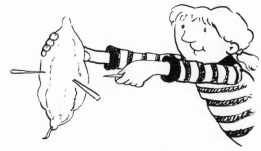

2. Fill the container almost full of water.
3. Put the narrow end of the sweet potato in the water. The rim of the container will support the toothpicks so that most of the sweet potato is not in the water.

4. Watch for signs of sprouting and keep track of how long your vine grows.

A suspicious beginning

The Spanish explorers didn't underestimate the value of the potato. It was one food that was easy to cook and easy to store. It kept well on long ocean voyages, and although the sailors didn't know about vitamins then (no one did), it soon became clear that the sailors who ate potatoes during their long trips didn't lose their teeth or suffer from bleeding gums and crooked bones. The potatoes were rich in vitamin C, which prevented the deadly disease called scurvy. Still, it wasn't until 1570 that the Spanish sailors brought the potatoes home to be planted.

The potato was not an instant success. It was a measly looking thing and people weren't sure what to do with it. Certainly there are records from as far back as 1573 telling of a hospital that used potatoes. But who knows if the patients liked them?

Italian sailors probably bought potatoes in Spain to plant at home since it was a novelty to grow weird new plants from exotic places such as Peru.

It was not long after that an ambassador to the Pope gave some potato seedlings to a famous botanist in Belgium. He grew more plants and then sent seedlings to friends across Europe. Most people didn't have a clue what to do with the new plant, so they grew it and then fed the lumpy, brown roots to the pigs!

From the West Indies to England

You might suspect that sailors brought potatoes from France or Holland to England. It was sailors, but the route was a little more complicated.

Sir Francis Drake gets the credit for bringing the first potatoes to England. He spent a lot of his time stealing gold from Spanish ships on their way home from the mines in South America. It was on one of these ships in the West Indies that Drake discovered potatoes in 1586. He brought some home and gave a few samples to his good friend, Sir Walter Raleigh, who lived near Cork, Ireland. It wasn't long before Sir Walter had a field of potatoes in Ireland. Some people think that Sir Walter Raleigh also planted potatoes in Roanoke, Virginia.

Sir Walter Raleigh

Actually, that's just a story. Sir Walter never even set foot in Virginia! And potatoes didn't come to America until much later.

Caviar, potatoes and poison

The potato was slow to catch on in the British Isles. In fact, the potato was such a rare and expensive item in the 1660s that only rich people could afford them.

Many of the people thought potatoes were an evil food. The people were very superstitious and believed that if they ate a potato, they would start to look like one! Nobody wanted wrinkly, dirty, lumpy skin.

Do you know that the slang word for potato, "spud," comes from a long narrow spade used to dig potatoes called — what else? — a spud?

What does a British potato say when it thinks something is wonderful? It's mashing!

Other people thought it was very suspicious that the potato grew underground. After all, the most beautiful fruits, such as apples and pears, had flowers and fruit in the clean, sun-filled air. Potatoes must be a sinful, dirty food to have to hide themselves so far underground. The Scottish people were devoutly religious, and they wouldn't eat potatoes because they weren't mentioned in the Bible. And in England in the early nineteenth century, most people thought that potatoes were an aphrodisiac — eating just one could make the most mild-mannered person extremely passionate.

It took some wars and some far-sighted philosophers to change the image of the potato and make it an important part of the European diet.

The patron of potatoes

In 1744, most of Europe was a battleground. Prussia, about where Germany is now, was constantly at war, which greatly distressed the country's ruler. Frederick the Great wrung his hands as he watched his people die of starvation. He knew about the potato from his travels and he was determined that his people would give up their superstitions against it and start eating this simple, nutritious food. The Prussians were already growing potatoes but they were feeding them to their cattle.

The ruler asked his royal cooks to invent new recipes that used potatoes and then he made sure each household in Prussia had copies of the recipes. But people still fed the potatoes to their livestock. Frederick would not stand back. He sent soldiers around the country with baskets of potatoes for planting. And then he laid down the law: either grow the potatoes and eat them...or have your ears cut off! Needless to say, the method worked.

Potatoes became the most important part of the Prussian diet. They were so popular by the time Prussia was at war with France during the Seven Year War (from 1756 to 1763), that everybody in the country was eating potatoes.

A French pharmacist named Auguste Parmentier was captured during this war and survived prison eating little more than potatoes. When he returned to France at the war's end, Parmentier

Parmentier

wanted every French family to feast on potatoes since he knew they could keep the people healthy. He went to the king with his plan to grow potatoes and feed the hungry. The king couldn't have been too enthusiastic — he gave Parmentier the worst land around Paris. It wouldn't grow anything and so was called Les Sablons — Sandy Plain. Like Frederick the Great, Parmentier used some persuasive, tricky ways to change public opinion about the potato.

The potatoes grew at Les Sablons despite the poor soil, just as Parmentier knew they would. He had been studying the potato and testing the best ways to grow it after he came back from prison. Knowing that the French countrymen would not want to eat the same food they fed pigs, Parmentier devised a plan. He would pretend the food was so precious that it must be guarded. But he told the soldiers to accept bribes and let the farmers "steal" the potatoes for planting. It worked: it seems people always want what they are told they cannot have.

But Parmentier didn't stop there: he threw a huge potato party. He invited the greatest names in France to a dinner in which all dishes, from the soups to the desserts, were made with potatoes! The queen even wore potato flowers in her hair. The plan was a success and the potato became socially acceptable. Even today, great chefs in France celebrate Parmentier with special dinners where the food, of course, is made from potatoes, and even the decorations feature the spud!

The great hunger

It was a dull, wet, cold summer in Ireland in 1845. The farmers grumbled about working until they were exhausted, while their bosses, fat, rich landlords, ate course after course of rich foods and spent their time at concerts and the theatre in London.

All the peasant families worked in the fields. And what did they earn? Each man, woman and child was paid just a sack of potatoes a day. Some of the lucky farmers owned a cow to give fresh milk (and guess what the cows ate for fodder) or a pig for slaughter. The Irish peasants ate potatoes for breakfast, lunch and supper. They even made a potato wine called poteen from the potato peelings. It was a simple, hard life with few surprises.

Then one day a farmer noticed a black spot on a leaf of one of his potato plants. "Wonder what that is?" he asked himself. How could he know that the dreaded black spot on his potato plant was the beginning of a blight that would devastate all the crops in Ireland and cause more

Potato blights

The potato blight that devastated Ireland during the Great Hunger was caused by a fungus that had threatened crops in the New World for years. It spread from New York to Canada around 1843. Scientists think that infected potatoes were then shipped to Europe, and the fungus went with them. Almost all the potato countries in the world were hurt, but Ireland was hardest hit because the peasants depended almost entirely on potatoes for their income and food.

The fungus has been around a long time and it looks as if it's here to stay.

It lays dormant in hot, dry weather and thrives on wet, cool weather late in the potato's growing cycle. Whenever the weather and the timing is right, the fungus attacks potato plants. Farmers know the symptoms now and can save crops by picking them early, or by spraying them with a special fungicide. But, so far, scientists haven't developed a blight-resistant potato.

than one million Irish people to die of sickness or starvation? In a country that survived on potatoes, suddenly there were none. There was no help for any of the poor farmers – no food and no money. There was nothing to do but die or leave.

Everybody was stunned. Nobody knew what was happening to the plants. The farmer fingering his blackened plants didn't know what was causing the problem. Was it a curse from God? Was it all the rain?

No, it couldn't be the rain, argued the experts. There had been wetter summers in Ireland and the crops had been good then. It must be those new electric generators, said others, afraid of the just invented power source. "It's not natural," they cried.

Science was in its infancy. Nobody understood that an unseen fungus was attacking the plants. The fungus spores were carried by the air. Once they landed on the plant, and the cold, wet rains helped them grab hold, they used the plant for food. The spores sprouted and the roots dug deep into the plant, sucking up the nutrients. In just a week, an infected plant would be black and dead.

Since the people of the time did not understand about microscopic diseases, they planted some surviving potatoes the next year. But they were infected and that crop failed, too. Ireland became a ghost land. The peasants either died or piled on filthy, disease-ridden ships bound for a promised better life in North America. The vessels were so terrible that they were called coffin ships because so many passengers died on board.

Make a mystery dessert

Only after your guests have oohhed and aaaahed and sighed, "Divine!" tell them that the secret ingredient is none other than mashed potatoes. Don't be put off by the mystery yourself… try it, you'll love it!

You'll need:

- a 2 L (9 x 5 inch) loaf pan
- waxed paper
- 5 28-g (1-oz) squares unsweetened chocolate
- 5 mL (1 tsp) instant coffee powder
- a double-boiler or microwave-proof bowl
- a medium-sized bowl
- an electric mixer
- 125 mL (½ cup) soft butter
- 375 mL (1½ cup) sugar
- 5 egg yolks
- 5 mL (1 tsp) vanilla or almond extract
- 500 mL (2 cups) hot mashed potatoes (fresh or instant)
- a spoon or spatula

1. Cover the inside of the loaf pan with waxed paper.
2. GET AN ADULT TO HELP you melt the chocolate and the coffee powder together in the double boiler or in the microwave. Remove from the heat to cool a bit after it's melted.

Did you know there was even a war named after potatoes? The *Kartoffelkrieg* was a war fought between the Prussians and the Austrians in 1778 – 79. In German, *Kartoffel* means potato and *Krieg* means war. When the Prussians attacked, they ate all the potatoes in the Austrian fields. When the Austrians attacked, they ate all the potatoes in the Prussian fields. The war was over when soldiers on both sides had no more potatoes to eat!

6. Add the melted chocolate and coffee to the bowl and beat until they are well blended with the other ingredients.

7. Add the potatoes and beat until well mixed.

8. Scoop the mystery delight into the baking pan. Cover the top with waxed paper and put in the refrigerator for 24 hours. Cut into 12 thin slices.

3. Put the butter in the bowl and beat it with the electric mixer until it is pale yellow and very creamy.

4. Slowly add the sugar and beat it until all the sugar is mixed into the butter.

5. Add the egg yolks and flavouring and beat until both are well mixed into the butter and sugar mixture.

Do you know that a potato once helped an infamous gangster escape prison? John Dillinger took a long potato and carved it in the shape of a gun. He dyed it black with iodine and convinced guards he was heavily armed! Either Dillinger was an artist in disguise, or the guards were in the wrong line of work!

Guess what was used for snowflakes in the movie *Close Encounters of the Third Kind*. Dried potato flakes.

Potatoes in the New World

Potatoes travelled from South America to North America in a roundabout way. Spanish explorers brought them to Europe, and colonial settlers carried some back across the Atlantic Ocean. The first potatoes in the English colonies were planted by Scottish and Irish pioneers in Londonderry, New Hampshire, in 1719. Still, the knobby little vegetable didn't become really popular until Irish immigrants arrived in large numbers after 1845.

Aroostock County, Maine, once had the record for producing the most potatoes in the U.S. That was before french fries and potato chips became so popular. Now, the honours have moved further west to Idaho, where the perfect french fry potato, the Russet Burbank, grows. The farms of Idaho produce over 100 million bags of potatoes every year, about one quarter of the U.S.A.'s crop. Second is neighboring Washington state, and then Maine.

In Canada, the governor of Prince Edward Island sent the first official report of a new potato crop to England in 1771. Only 19 years later, after the American Revolution, there were so many potatoes on the Island that farmers were exporting them to nearby Nova Scotia and New Brunswick. Today, this tiny island grows one-third of all the country's potatoes—more than 820 million kilograms (1800 million pounds)—a year. The warm days, cool nights, iron-rich, red soil and ample rain make perfect potato crop conditions.

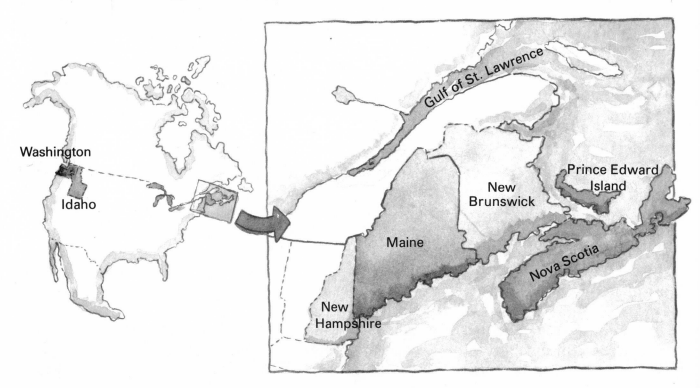

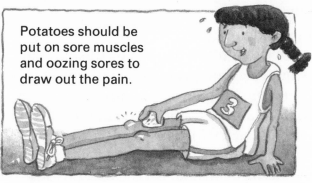

Potatoes should be put on sore muscles and oozing sores to draw out the pain.

A potato in your pocket will cure rheumatism and eczema.

If you boil some potatoes, keep the water because you can use it to darken your hair, clean silverware or keep leather shoes and jackets soft and clean!

If you have a wart, rub it with a cut potato, then bury the potato. As the potato rots in the ground, your wart will disappear!

Myths and miracles

It seems that people either love or hate potatoes. Depending on where you live, you may think potatoes can perform miracles or bring bad luck or even tragedy. What do you think about these old (and some not-so-old!) beliefs about potatoes?

If you dump a pot of boiled potatoes on a farmer's field, the potatoes in the field will turn rotten.

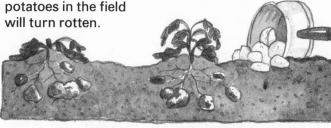

If a woman is expecting a baby, she should not eat potatoes because the baby will be born with a big head!

Made some enemies lately? In Italy, people would print the name of their enemy on a piece of paper and, using as many pins as possible, pin the note to the potato. It was said that an enemy cursed this way would suffer a painful, fast death.

Celebrate a festival

Some time in December each year, Jewish children around the world celebrate Chanukah (HAH-na-ka). During the eight-day-long festival, the children go to parties, play special games and eat special foods.

Chanukah celebrates a miracle that happened during a war more than 2000 years ago. The Syrian people had taken over a sacred Jewish temple in Jerusalem. But a group of Hebrew soldiers led by Judah Maccabee won the temple back. Maccabee and his followers wanted to purify the temple after it had been invaded and dedicate it again to God. They could find only one jar of sacred oil for the holy temple light, the menorah. There was hardly enough oil for even one day. They poured it into the menorah and lit it. Miraculously, the oil burned for eight days.

Jewish families remember the miracle by lighting candles in a special candle holder each Chanukah. The candle holder has places for eight candles and a special place for a shammus (worker) candle. On each day of the festival, candles are burned. On the first day just before sundown, one candle is lit. By the end of the festival, all eight candles are lit.

The food is especially wonderful at Chanukah. A favourite dish is potato pancakes, or latkes (LAT-kas), which are fried in oil. Each family has its own treasured recipe for latkes. Try this version, but please remember that hot oil is dangerous. You must do the frying with an adult.

You can make latkes any time, but they have a special meaning during Chanukah.

You'll need:
  a colander
  a medium bowl
  a potato peeler
  6 medium potatoes
  a grater
  1 large onion
  1 egg
  a fork
  50 mL (¼ cup) milk
  125 mL (½ cup) flour
  5 mL (1 tsp) salt
  pepper
  oil for frying

  a heavy frying pan
  an ice-cream scoop
  a pancake flipper
  paper towels
  applesauce or sour cream

1. Sit the colander in the bowl. Peel the potatoes then grate them into the colander.

2. Squish down the potatoes with your hands so any liquid is squeezed out. Let the potatoes stand for about 10 minutes, then squish again. Lift the colander up and throw out any water in the bowl. Put the grated potatoes into the bowl.

3. Grate the onion and add it to the potatoes.

4. Beat the egg with the fork. Add the egg, milk, flour, salt and pepper to the potatoes.

5. Stir everything very well.

6. Pour enough oil into the pan so that it covers the bottom of the pan. Heat the oil **with the help of an adult**.

7. For each pancake you'll need enough batter to fill the ice-cream scoop. Place the scoopful of batter in the pan and flatten it with the flipper. Make about three pancakes at a time. Turn each pancake once when the bottom turns a golden brown. When the pancakes are brown all over, put them on a sheet of paper towel to drain the cooking oil.

8. Serve the pancakes with applesauce or sour cream. This recipe serves three latke fanatics or six latke lovers.

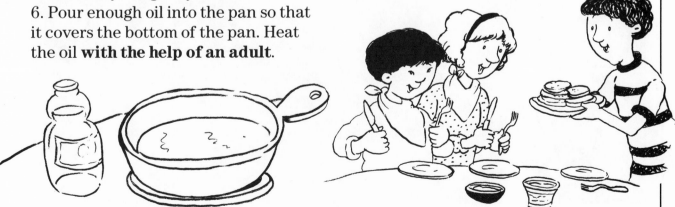

A POTATO TALE

*Storytellers around the world have their
own versions of this tale about a
poor farmer and a rich, greedy farmer.
If you tell this story around a
campfire, you're carrying on a fine,
old tradition.*

Once a long, long time ago, there were two farmers. Poor Jack went to Big Fred, the wealthiest, greediest farmer around, and asked to rent some land.

Big Fred thought about it and said, "All right. But only if we share."

"Share what?" asked Poor Jack.

"Well, I take the top of the crop for my share and you take the bottom."

Poor Jack agreed and as soon as he left Big Fred slapped his thighs and laughed out loud. He knew Poor Jack had made a poor bargain. Everybody knows the crops are on the top and the bottom is only roots.

Poor Jack ploughed and planted and weeded until it was time to bring in the crop.

"We've got a fine crop, Big Fred," he

said. "You better come take your share, because I'm ready to dig my potatoes."

Big Fred looked at the field of wilted potato plants and swore Poor Jack would never outsmart him again.

So the next year when he rented the land he told Poor Jack he wanted the bottoms this time.

Poor Jack ploughed and planted and weeded until it was time to bring in the crop.

"We've got a fine crop, Big Fred," he said. "I've taken all my oats from the top. What do you want to do with your straw from the bottom?"

Big Fred was hopping mad.

"Next year," he shouted. "I'm going to take the tops and the bottoms!"

"What does that leave me?" asked Poor Jack, scratching his head. Big Fred chuckled when he answered, "The middle, of course."

Big Fred was sure he'd outsmarted Poor Jack this time. But Jack went out and ploughed and planted and weeded until it was time to bring in the crop. When Big Fred looked at the field and saw what was growing, he screamed.

Poor Jack had planted corn. Big Fred got the stalks and the tassels and Poor Jack got the cobs.

The next year Jack and Fred struck a new deal. They each got half of everything and Jack wasn't poor anymore.

33

Make a handy hand heater

Football fans in cold stadiums have found a way to warm their hands during freezing late-season football games and have a cheap, nutritious snack as well. They make hot potato hand heaters.

It's easy, so why don't you try to make your own hand heater before heading out to the skating rink or ski hill.

You'll need:

a baking potato – Russet is the best
a fork
a table knife
toppings – try cheese slices, bacon bits, butter, chives, or whatever you like
enough aluminum foil to wrap twice around the potato

1. Preheat oven to 220° C (425° F).
2. Wash, scrub and dry the potato. Pierce it in a couple of places with the fork.

3. Put the potato directly on the oven rack and bake for 1¼ hours or until the entire potato feels soft.
4. Cut a large X in the top of the potato. Put in the toppings you like.

5. Wrap the potato in foil. Put the potato in your pocket and hold whenever your hand needs warming up. Eat it when you're hungry!

Do you know that there is a museum devoted just to potatoes? It got its start in Belgium in 1975 but is now housed in Washington, D.C. The curators, Tom and Meredith Hughes, have collected more than 2500 items, such as songs, stamps and posters, all about potatoes, and equipment such as peelers and mashers. People even subscribe to their potato magazine called, appropriately, *Peelings*!

The name game

When *papas* were first described by a conquistador travel writer in 1553, they were compared to a round, underground mushroom called a truffle. *Papas* aren't anything like truffles, but the name stuck. Perhaps English-speaking people today would be calling potatoes truffles, except when *papas* first reached Europe someone confused them with sweet potatoes, *batatas*. *Papas* became *patatas* and that translated into potatoes in English.

Can you match each country shown on this map with the local word for potato? (You'll find the names in the box at the bottom of the page.) Here are some hints to help you: two of the names are used in more than one country and another name is the name used by scientists around the world.

Then follow the paths that the potato took around the world to become popular. (Answers on page 64.)

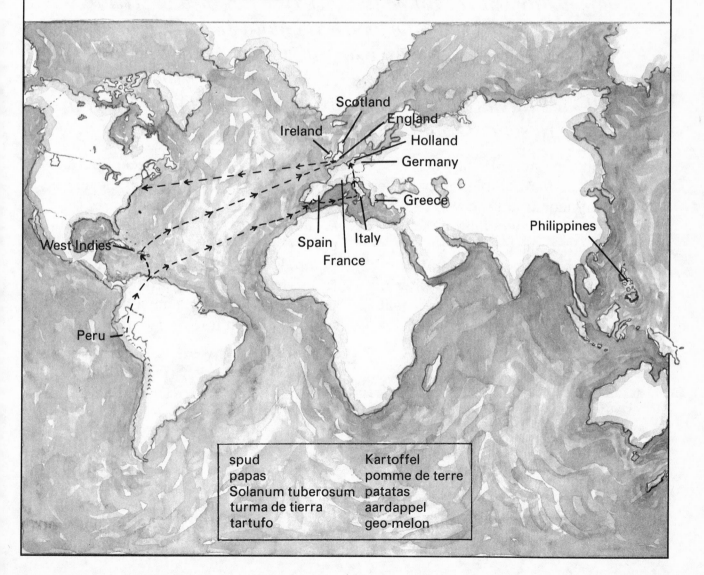

spud	Kartoffel
papas	pomme de terre
Solanum tuberosum	patatas
turma de tierra	aardappel
tartufo	geo-melon

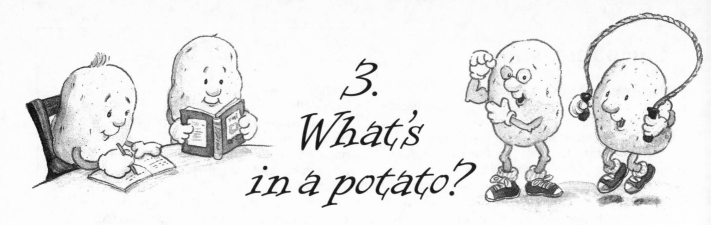

3. What's in a potato?

For a starving child in the Philippines or a destitute family in India, a new food — the potato — could mean the difference between life and death. Poor, hungry children in Peru who are fed mashed potatoes with milk, vitamins and a little butter or oil are performing better in school and becoming stronger and healthier.

Scientists at the International Potato Centre in Lima, Peru, think that potatoes may solve hunger around the world!

Most of the world depends on rice, wheat and corn to make its everyday foods. But the experts say that potatoes are cheaper, easier and faster to grow and they're more nutritious than rice, wheat or corn. Potatoes can be grown almost anywhere in the world — except perhaps in the centre of a desert or in the middle of a rainforest.

Just think how wonderful it would be if every country in the world could grow potatoes and feed its hungry. Scientists think that is possible with new types of potatoes. By now, you must be wondering what's in this miracle vegetable, anyway?

Wonder food

If you were stranded on a desert island, and you could have only two things with you, what would you want?

You couldn't go wrong with a ·basket of potatoes and a cow to produce fresh milk. If you stored just half of the potatoes and planted the rest, you would have enough healthy food to feed you for one year—and serve a banquet to the crew of your rescue ship!

Just two potatoes a day will give you all the vitamin C you need. As well, each potato contains water, protein, fat, carbohydrates, calcium, phosphorus, iron, sodium, potassium, vitamin A, thiamine, riboflavin, niacin, vitamin B_6, copper, magnesium, iodine, folic acid and zinc. *Whew!!* No wonder potatoes are seen as the solution to nutrition problems around the world!

Open wide!
What's a dentist's favourite vegetable? The potato—because people who eat potatoes as the main part of their diet have fewer cavities in their teeth. Potatoes don't stick to your teeth and the rough skin fibres give your teeth a little scrub with every bite.

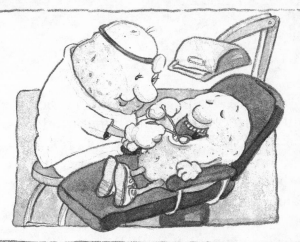

Vitamin P?
The potato is a medical miracle. The vitamin C in it cures scurvy. The vitamin B_1 (thiamine) prevents both dropsy, a terrible illness where fluid collects in the cavities and tissues of the body, and beriberi, a crippling nerve disease. The vitamin B_3 (niacin) in potatoes prevents pellagra, a disease that can cause terrible depression.

Inside the potato

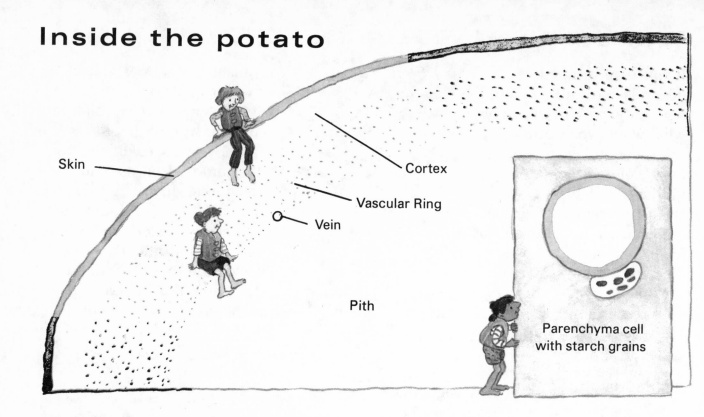

Skin

Cortex

Vascular Ring

Vein

Pith

Parenchyma cell
with starch grains

If you were shrunk as tiny as a microchip and inserted into a potato, what would you find? Well, first you'd better cross your fingers and hope that you don't land in the centre of the potato unless you are wearing a microchip-sized life jacket. The centre of a potato is called the pith, but to a shrunken kid it could be called the Great Sea because all the potato's water is stored in the cells here. Almost 80% of the potato's weight is water.

Make your way over to the edge and hoist yourself up. You're probably sitting on the vascular ring. This ring goes around the pith, but there are so many tiny veins that you might get confused if you tried to walk around it. Instead, take a rest and watch the glucose surge through the veins on its way down from the leaves. Check

out that tiny cell beside you. It's called a parenchyma cell and soon it will be filled with grains of starch.

Keep on moving towards the outer edge of the potato. Now you're in the cortex, the narrow band that contains almost one-third of the nutrients of the potato. You're near the end of your journey now. Feel that thick, rough bit on the outer edge? That's the potato skin. It protects the potato while the potato's growing and keeps moisture inside. The older the potato, the tougher the skin.

Break through the potato's skin and you're out. Time to grow, grow, grow! Grab a potato chip and take a close look at it. Can you name the darker ring near the outside edge?

Right! It's the cortex.

The best potato for the job

If you are lucky enough to travel to Peru, go to the market where the native farmers sell their goods. There on blankets on the ground, you'll see baskets filled with potatoes the colours of jewels. You might not even recognize the vegetables as potatoes since they don't look anything like North American or European potatoes.

There are more than 5000 different kinds of potatoes in the Andes. Some are long and knobby, others look like corkscrews; some are U-shaped and others are shaped like green peppers. They can be purple or ivory, ruby red or golden. There are so many shapes, sizes and colours of potatoes that the Quechua Indian language has 1000 different words for potato. Some of the words are very descriptive: a potato that is hard and knobbly and very difficult to peel is called "lumchipamundana." Translated into English, that means, "potato makes young bride weep."

In North America, there is very little variety in potatoes. Most farmers grow only eight different types because they want to make sure their potatoes are sold. Since most potatoes are sold to big companies that make potato chips, french fries, instant potatoes and hash-browns, farmers grow the varieties that the companies will buy.

The big companies know exactly what kind of potatoes make the best "baker"— the long, thin Russet potato that grows perfectly in Idaho, Washington, and Canada's Maritime provinces. The Russet makes the best french fries, too. Why? Because it is easy to cut into long strips and is high in starch so it doesn't get brown too quickly, doesn't absorb too much cooking oil and stays fluffy!

Farmers' favourites

In North America, farmers prefer these categories of potatoes:

Russet
(such as Russet Burbank, Norgold Russet)

Round White
(such as Kennebec, Sebago)

Red
(such as Red LaSoda, Chieftain)

Yellow-Fleshed
(such as Yukon Gold, Bintje)

Hold the starch

Potatoes are made mostly of water and starch. There's a good reason for that. Potatoes may grow underground like carrots and parsnips, but unlike them, they are not a root vegetable. They are a tuber. A what? A tuber is a bulge in the plant's rhizome. The plant's what? A rhizome is an underground part of a plant's stem that is used to store extra food.

When a potato plant is growing, the leaves make lots of food called glucose.

But there comes a time after the first "growth spurt" when the plant makes too much glucose to use right away. The extra glucose is sent down the stem and into the end of the rhizome. When glucose is stored, the little glucose molecules clump together to form a grain of starch. As the plant stores more starch, the tip of the rhizome gets longer and rounder until it forms a tuber. You know tubers by another name — potato.

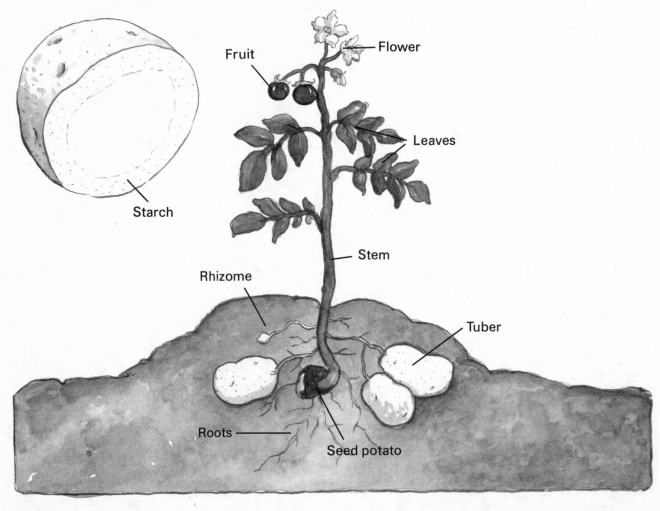

Fruit

Flower

Leaves

Starch

Stem

Rhizome

Tuber

Roots

Seed potato

But does it do the backstroke?

There are hundreds of types of potatoes, all with different shapes, sizes, colours and textures. But when you get right down to it, there are two main types: high starch and low starch. Table potatoes are low in starch and stay firm when you boil them or put them in soups and stews. Baking potatoes have lots of starch and they get fluffy when they're baked, mashed or made into french fries.

You don't have to be a potato farmer to figure out which kind of potato you have in your kitchen cupboard. You can do this easy experiment.

You'll need:
  250 mL (1 cup) salt
  3 L (11 cups) water
  a large bowl
  different looking potatoes — try a red-skinned potato, a long, brown potato and a Yukon Gold potato

1. Pour the salt and water into the bowl.
2. Try floating the potatoes in the water. Watch which potatoes sink and which potatoes float.

Scientists would say you have just discovered which potatoes have higher specific gravity. That's a way of saying how much things weigh when they are in water. High-starch potatoes have a higher specific gravity than low-starch potatoes.

Try the experiment with plain water. Does it work? Does salt make it easier to float objects in water?

Where's the starch?

Now that you know potatoes contain starch, where is it? You can tell where the potato stores starch by doing this simple test.

You'll need:
  a table knife
  a potato
  a small brush
  brown tincture of iodine (available at a drugstore)

1. Cut the potato in half.

2. Look at the knife. The whitish liquid on it is starch.
3. Brush the surface of the potato slice with iodine.
4. Wherever there is starch, the iodine turns from brown to purple.

Are there some parts of the potato where there is more starch stored than in other parts? Try the experiment using a baking potato and a table potato. Can you see any differences? Try putting a potato in the fridge overnight and then do the experiment.

Potato unscramble

These are all potato words but they're a little mixed up. Can you sort them out?

(Answers on page 64.)

HSAMDE SOPRTU LEEP

PCHI CHRAST

EPI OADHI

VSAHRET

EURP STSURE

Potato bags

You've heard of potato sacks, right? They're the burlap bags that contain potatoes. But you probably haven't heard of potato bags – they're bags that look like regular plastic bags but they're made from potato starch.

Most plastic bags are made from petroleum and they last forever. If you buried a plastic bag today, it would still look the same 100 years from now. These bags don't disintegrate or become part of the soil and so they make a lot of garbage.

Scientists have been searching for new materials that are strong but easy to get rid of without hurting the environment. A group of experts in New Jersey discovered that when they heated potato starch, it made a sticky liquid. When the liquid cooled, it looked and acted just like plastic. And here's the best part: potato "plastic" is made

from carbon and oxygen that breaks down into harmless carbon dioxide and water when it's buried.

Soon, there may be toys and other products made from this potato starch "plastic."

Turn a Potato Green

Unless you grow potatoes in your garden, you've probably never seen a potato plant leaf or potato seeds. The leaf looks a little like its cousin, the tobacco leaf, and the seeds look like little green tomatoes (another relative!). But don't chew the leaves or nibble on the fruit. There's a skeleton in this family closet—the Deadly Nightshade plant. Potato leaves and fruit are filled with a natural, poisonous pesticide called solanine, the same poison in Deadly Nightshade.

When a potato is dug up from underground or pulled out of a potato sack, it is not at all poisonous. But if you leave it in sunshine, it can turn from a perfectly palatable potato to a poisonous one. It's unlikely you would die from eating a bit of green potato, but the potato would taste bad and you could get very sick. Here's an experiment to see the potato turn green.

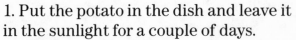

You'll need:
a potato
a dish
a sunny place

1. Put the potato in the dish and leave it in the sunlight for a couple of days.
2. Watch to see if your potato turns green.

Inside the potato there are small oval cells called parenchyma cells. These look white and each have a grain of starch inside. When a potato is put in sunshine, these parenchyma cells get a message to change jobs. Instead of storing starch, they start manufacturing chlorophyll and turn into green chloroplasts. The chlorophyll in a potato plant contains the solanine poison.

There's a good lesson in this experiment. If you grow potatoes, make sure they never see light. And, if you store potatoes, make sure they are in a dry, dark place.

Potato sayings

Small potatoes!
If your sister says the money you collected for a school project is "small potatoes" she deserves a dirty look. She's saying that the amount is insignificant.

Hot potato
A hot potato is a problem or an issue that nobody wants to deal with or talk about.

Potato prints charming

Oh, no! The birthday party starts in two hours and there's no wrapping paper in the house. Here's how to make your own designer paper and create a sensation. It's a great way to recycle paper too!

You'll need:
  a kitchen knife
  a potato
  a marking pen
  paper towel or old cloth
  newspaper
  tempera or poster paint
  a small plastic container
  a piece of paper – any type and size
    you like

1. Carefully slice the potato in half width-wise.

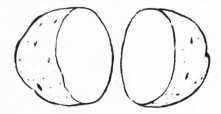

2. Use a marking pen to draw a simple design on the smooth side of one potato half. (Save the other half.) Try drawing stars, circles, hearts or lines.

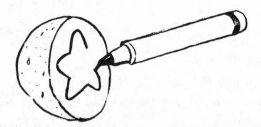

3. Cut around the outside lines of the design. Carve away the potato until the design stands up about 1 cm (½ inch). Dry the cut edge with a towel.

4. Cover your work area with newspaper. Pour the paint into the containers.

5. Dip the cut edge of the potato into the paint. Make sure your entire stamp is covered but not dripping with paint. Press the potato "stamp" firmly onto the paper. Repeat and make a random design or make a pattern on the paper.

You can make your wrapping paper more interesting by printing in two or three different colours and overlapping the designs. You could even make two different stamps with each half of the potato and make a dynamic design. Why not try fabric paint and make your unique stamp on a hat, T-shirt or underwear?

Mr. Potato Head

When Mr. Potato Head was first invented, he consisted of a potato sack filled with plastic parts including sunglasses, shoes, hats, various sizes of ears, eyes, glasses and a pipe. Kids had to supply their own potato for the body. But moms were soon complaining because the kids kept forgetting where they put their potato heads. Later, the potatoes would be found stinking and rotting under beds and behind radiators.

The next generation of Mr. Potato Head came with a plastic potato body and parts that allowed kids to make a Ms. Potato Head and "sprouts." In the most recent generation of the Potato Head Family, there is no longer a pipe, since smoking is hazardous. Instead, kids can make the Potato Head Family look pretty zany with new headgear such as snorkels!

You can make your own potato people the old-fashioned way.

You'll need:
    a potato
    a kitchen knife
    fruits, vegetables and herbs
    toothpicks

1. Use the potato for a body and make the face, arms, legs, etc., by attaching pieces of carrot, celery, apple, etc., with the toothpicks.

2. Make hair from parsley, dill or carrot tops.

For a change, try making animals out of the potatoes. Four stubs of carrot and a fiddlehead make the wonderful beginning of a potato pig. There's only one problem: eventually, your potato masterpiece will shrivel and rot. Throw out your creation before it starts to stink! Or you could make potato people and animals from baked or boiled potatoes and eat them for dinner.

4. Dig that hoe

The next time you reach into a potato bag and pull out a weird lump that is slightly shrivelled and studded with thick white shoots and wiggly white roots, don't screech. It's not an alien being about to take over your home! It's a sprouting tuber.

How potatoes grow

When you look closely, you'll notice that the shoots grow only from certain spots on the potato. Those spots, or indents, are called eyes and the curve on top of each one is called, no kidding, an eyebrow.

Inside each eye are several buds. When the potato starts to grow, the buds develop into thick, white sprouts with a cluster of folded leaves at the tip. Each sprout becomes the stem and leaves of a new potato plant. At the base of each sprout are long white threads. These are the roots of the potato plant and the rhizomes. The root hairs absorb water and food from the earth and the roots send the food and water up to the leaves. The rhizome will start to swell when the plant has finished most of its growing. Remember, it's the rhizome that becomes the part you eat, the tuber.

If you planted your sprouting potato deep into the ground, kept it watered and covered in earth as it grew, you'd have a nice plateful of potatoes in about three months. If you peeked under the ground a little early, you could pick a few new potatoes — they're small with thin skin that easily rubs off between your fingers.

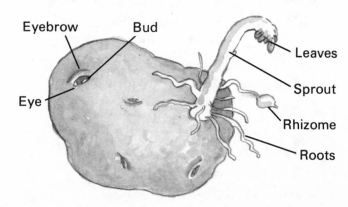

46

Brrrrrrr...don't chill your potatoes

You can stop your potatoes from sprouting by keeping them in a dark place at about 7° to 10° C (44° to 50° F) for up to three months. If you keep your potatoes longer, they may rot, and if you keep your potatoes in a warmer place, they may sprout. Take a clue from the old-timers who stored their potatoes in cool, dry, dark root cellars. But don't put your potatoes in the fridge. Below 4° C (38° F), the starch in your tuber turns to sugar. A sugary potato does not taste sweet, it tastes... well, disgusting.

Most potatoes sold in stores today are coated with a chemical that prevents sprouting. Even so, the best eating potatoes are the ones that have been stored properly.

Seeds that aren't for planting

Most vegetables and fruits can be grown from seed. You've probably planted seeds and grown vegetables such as carrots, peas and beans. So why don't you plant potato seeds when you want a potato? There's an answer, but it's going to take a little explaining.

There *are* potato seeds. They are formed like all seeds. After the stem and leaves have grown on a potato plant, and the tuber underground is getting bigger, the plant blossoms. Most potato plants have white flowers with sunshine yellow stamens, but some have brilliant purple or mauve flowers.

Bees travel from potato flower to potato flower, searching for nectar to drink. Sticky pollen from the flowers' stamens sticks to the bee's hairy legs. When the bee stops at the next plant to drink, some of the pollen drops off on the flower's pistil.

The pollen contains sperm. It travels down the pistil to the ovary, which contains ovules with tiny egg cells. When the sperm joins with the egg cells, a seed starts to grow. The ovary gets bigger and rounder and becomes the potato fruit. It looks like a green cherry tomato, and each one contains as many as 200 seeds. Farmers call these potato seeds T.P.S.— true potato seed.

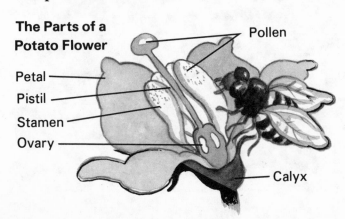

The Parts of a Potato Flower

Pollen

Petal

Pistil

Stamen

Ovary

Calyx

47

Eye of newt, potato fruit...

People do not eat the small green fruit of the potato plant with good reason: it's poisonous. The word must have gotten around since the last known case of death by potato poisoning was in 1933.

Actually, it's not all that easy to find potato plants bearing true potato seed. Plant breeders have found a way of producing plants that have no seed, and many farmers grow these since they don't use the true potato seed for anything, anyway.

When nature is left alone, the potato fruit falls to the ground in fall and the seeds are planted ready for the spring growing season. Or animals eat the fruit and then drop the seeds in dung in a new place. Next spring, a new potato plant pushes out of the ground, and the growing cycle starts all over again.

But what kind of potatoes grow when nature is left alone? Anything grows! The potatoes could have their mother's eyes and their father's shape! Or worse, they could look like a long-lost relative that resembled a black and purple corkscrew! That's not what farmers want and certainly not what the potato-chip makers and french-fry makers want. Farmers and manufacturers need to know exactly what kind of potatoes they are growing.

In South America there are more than 5000 different types of potatoes since they are allowed to grow wild. Centuries ago, the Andean Indians grew their potatoes from seeds and kept all the tubers for eating. But in North America, we do not let potatoes grow wild from "true seed." Instead farmers use specially grown potatoes called seed potatoes to start a new crop.

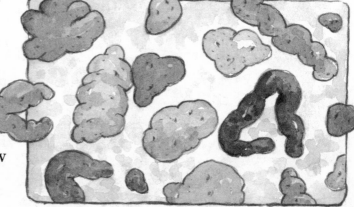

Potato clones

Seed potatoes are whole potatoes or chunks of potato with an eye that are planted to grow new potato plants. The tubers that are produced by the plant are exactly like their parent – they're clones.

It is vital that seed potatoes be free of bugs and diseases. If they are infected, a whole field of potatoes could be ruined. Those poor Irish potato farmers during the Great Hunger kept planting infected potatoes! Farmers know that when they buy "Certified Seed Potatoes" – they come mostly from Holland, Prince Edward Island and New Brunswick – that the seed potatoes have no diseases.

Government inspectors make sure seed potatoes are grown under strict, sterile conditions. At one of the largest potato seed farms in North America, the Elite Farm on Fox Island (connected to Prince Edward Island by a causeway), the trucks have to drive through a ditch of disinfectant before they enter the seed potato fields, just in case the dirt on the wheels of the truck is infected.

Farmers who grow seed potatoes have to disinfect their clothes and shoes before they walk into a seed potato field. When seed potato farmers greet each other they don't say, "Howdy," they say, "Have you washed your feet?"

A real cut-up

The natives in Peru discovered that a potato cut into pieces with eyes made more crops than a whole potato. Until the beginning of the last century, farmers cut potatoes into pieces with sharp knives. Then an inventor who wanted to speed up the cutting and cut down on the work made the pedal-powered Eureka seed cutter. A farmer sat on the cutter, pushed a lever with his foot and watched as a couple of knives sliced up the potato.

About 40 years later, an electric machine was invented to cut the potatoes. The operator put the potatoes onto a conveyor belt with spaces for different-sized potatoes and the belt ran under a set of knives. This machine was better because it was faster and better designed to cut big as well as small potatoes.

But all seed potato cutting machines share a big problem: if a potato with a disease is cut by a knife, the disease can live on the knife and enter a clean potato when it is cut. Now the big potato farms try to stay away from cutting and plant mostly small whole seed potatoes.

Test-tube potatoes

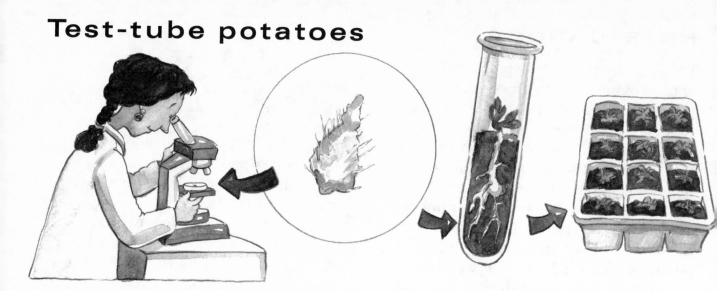

Farmers and scientists want to make sure that the potatoes they plant are healthy. Sometimes, when a potato is sick, it is covered in scabs and dots or has black sores or worse. But some viruses are invisible and there is no way to see if the potato is sick.

To solve this problem, scientists make test-tube potatoes. They cut the eye out of a healthy-looking potato, then they peel away the outer layers and put what's left under a microscope. Next, the scientist carefully cuts into the centre and pulls out a tiny, white bud. It is as small as the head of a pin. But that little dot contains everything that is needed to grow a potato plant! It is called a meristem.

The meristems are heat-treated to kill any diseases, then planted in a closed test tube with a special jelly that contains all the nutrients needed to grow a potato plant. When the seedlings have grown, they are tested to make sure they are healthy.

The scientist then cuts the plants into pieces that will root and grow. These tiny plants grow in greenhouses until they go to farmers in remote areas such as northern Ontario to produce a crop. (There's less chance of contaminated soil if the farm is far away from other farms.) The potatoes from these crops are planted in other government-inspected fields. Eventually, the seed potatoes that got their start under a microscope are called safe – "Certified" – and are sent to farmers around the world.

One tiny bit of a bud can be the parent to hundreds of thousands of clones. At one laboratory in Prince Edward Island, the scientists kept cutting the seedlings grown from one potato eye. In just one year, it made 1 tonne (1 ton) of potatoes!

Do you know that if you planted a potato that has just been dug up, it would not sprout? Potatoes have a dormant time when they will not grow.

Potatoes, potatoes everywhere

Potatoes grow in almost all of the 171 countries around the world. Only corn grows in more places. In one year, the world grows enough potatoes to cover a four-lane highway that would circle the world six times!

You might think that North America rates the highest in potato production. Actually, the Soviet Union grows most of the world's potatoes, followed by Poland, the United States and Canada.

In some countries, such as the Philippines and India, potatoes are regarded as a rare treat. Only rich families can afford to eat potatoes. A person in the Philippines who wants to show off at the grocery store might put a few potatoes on the top of his basket to indicate that he can afford luxuries.

Do you know that a new potato doesn't have to be a young or small potato? A new potato is any potato that hasn't spent time in storage!

Do you know that knobbly potatoes are formed when the weather changes from dry to wet? When the soil dries out completely, the potato stops growing. When the soil gets wet, the potato starts growing and makes a knob.

Ancient Peru

Often Indians let potato plants grow from seed, or they dug a hole with a *taclla* (foot-plough) and hand-planted a seed potato. They covered the potatoes with earth until a hill was made. Then they waited for rain and hoped the plants would grow. At the end of the

season, when the leaves and stem of the plants died, they dug up the potatoes by hand or, using the *taclla*, ripped off the dying vines and shook off the dirt. They piled the potatoes into sacks and slung them on the backs of llamas to be carried home.

Today

A gas-powered planter makes a trough, gently drops in the potato, deposits fertilizer on either side of the potato and makes a hill of earth on top of the planted seed potatoes.

Airplanes or machines spray chemicals to kill bugs and diseases.

The plants are killed when it's time for harvesting to make it easier for the machines to work. Harvesting machines pick eight rows of potatoes at a time. They cut off the vine, lift the potatoes out of the ground, separate the earth and stones from the potatoes and load the potatoes by conveyer belt into a truck.

Building a better potato

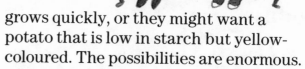

Any guesses about what a pomato or a topotato is? You're right — it's a cross between a tomato plant and a potato plant. This new plant, invented in Germany, grows tomatoes on top and potatoes underground! That's just one of the amazing things scientists are doing with potatoes.

Scientists know that when they plant a seed potato, they get a clone of the original potato. But they can use genetic engineering to make special potatoes from true potato seeds. The scientists grow the seeds from potato plants that have the qualities they want. They pollinate the plants with each other until they grow a potato that has all the features they are looking for; perhaps they want a potato high in starch that grows quickly, or they might want a potato that is low in starch but yellow-coloured. The possibilities are enormous.

Scientists usually create new varieties because the big potato-processing companies want to make their work easier. For instance, there's no sense growing round potatoes for french-fries — a long potato is needed. Also, there's no sense growing a potato that absorbs a lot of cooking oil when people are cutting down on the amount of fat they are eating. Farmers and store owners want potatoes that resist disease and pests and stay fresh a long time. Scientists are working to make potatoes with all those qualities.

Potato inventions

The age of the machine dawned for farmers around 1850. Everybody was making labour-saving devices because farms were getting bigger and it was too much work to do all the planting, harrowing and harvesting by hand. Besides, a new material, cast iron, made it possible to make bigger, better, longer-lasting machines.

By 1920, there were mechanical potato planters. The farmer sat on the front steering the horses and a worker sat in back to make sure the machine picked up seed potatoes out of a seed box and dropped them into the ground. However,

the machines were unreliable.

The improvements weren't much better. The Aspinwall-Picker Finger Planter grabbed the potatoes so tightly that it punctured them, crushed them and made it easier for disease to spread.

By 1940, there was a machine that picked up the potatoes with a small cup, dropped them into the ground, spread fertilizer along the side and mounded earth on top. Everybody was happy — including the potatoes.

A year on a pioneer potato farm

In 1816, Captain William Ross and his wife Mary moved from Ireland to Nova Scotia. There, they had seven children, including a son named Edward, who helped his father farm. Edward kept a diary and today that diary lets everyone know what life was really like in Nova Scotia in the 1800s. For the Ross family, the year revolved around potatoes.

January
The family ate potatoes stored in the underground cellar.

February
Edward had to make a fire in the cellar to keep the potatoes from freezing.

March and April
Down in the cellar, Edward picked through the potatoes to throw out the bad ones and find the sprouting potatoes.

May
Edward and his father cut seed potatoes by hand.

June
They burned the land to clear the weeds. Men, women and children carried seed potatoes in sacks on their shoulders and used a spade to dig holes for planting the potatoes.

July and August
They used scufflers to dig out weeds and hillers to make hills on top of the growing tubers. The Rosses probably picked off bugs with their fingers and killed them. There were no chemicals to kill diseases.

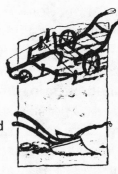

September
The family uncovered some new potatoes with a spade and ate them!

October
The entire family helped dig potatoes and put them into baskets woven by local native people. The potatoes were loaded into barrels for storage.

November and December
The Rosses picked through the potatoes. Rotten ones were fed to livestock.

Getting the bugs out

It's not only people who love potatoes. The potato plant is the number one luncheon choice for the Colorado Potato Beetle. It would go almost anywhere for a nibble of potato leaf. The story of the travelling Colorado Potato Beetle shows just how persistent this pesky pest is.

In 1824 the CPB, as the experts call it, lived cosily in Colorado eating a plant called buffalo bur. As soon as the settlers planted potatoes, the CPB started eating the leaves. "Fantastic!" the beetles cried.

Female CPBs can lay an egg every two minutes! That's a lot of hungry beetles. They started flying east in search of more food and gobbled every potato leaf along the way. By the spring of 1871, they had crossed the Mississippi and were heading east and north devouring crops. The CPBs hopped rides on anything that floated. Every couple of years, they hit a new town, a new state or a new province. It's believed they even hitchhiked to Europe along with potatoes being sent to soldiers in the First World War.

This nasty bug destroys crops but it is very difficult to destroy. Farmers have designed machines that smother them with dust and drown them in oil but the beetle keeps reappearing.

There's one good thing about the CPB — they are big and slow so kids can pick 'em and kill 'em and in some places get paid a penny a beetle!

Getting rid of the nasties nicely

It's not only bugs that bug potato farmers! Potatoes are prone to fungus, virus and bacterial infections. The wind carries fungus spores that attack the leaves and stems of plants. From plant to plant, insects carry viruses that can stop the tuber growing or make the tubers funny shapes and colours. People, machines and other plants exchange bacterial infections that can make tubers rot. It's a battleground out there on the potato field!

Farmers have to handle each problem in a special way. They can plant certified seed to make sure their seed potatoes are free from disease right from the start. They can destroy diseased plants and spray the plants and earth with chemicals to kill diseases.

Scientists keep developing new potato varieties that resist potato diseases and bugs. And farmers keep searching for methods to control pests that are natural and don't harm the environment. There's even a machine available that vacuums pests right off the plant!

Grow a potato

Don't throw away a potato with eyes that are sprouting. That potato's ready to be planted. It's easy to grow your own delicious fresh potatoes.

Try cutting your sprouting potato into quarters so that each piece has an eye. Put the pieces onto a plate with water and keep them wet for at least one week. Does each piece sprout?

If you want garden potatoes, follow these instructions in the spring.

1. Buy seed potatoes from a garden store or find some potatoes that are sprouting.
2. In the garden, use a hoe to dig a V-shaped ditch 15 cm (6 inches) deep.

3. Drop your seed potato into the ditch every 22 cm (9 inches).

4. Fill in the ditch with soil. Water well.
5. Every two weeks, pile more dirt up on your potato ditch. This ensures that the potatoes are well covered as the plant grows.

6. After two or three months, the potato plant will bloom. In another two weeks or so, the leaves and stem start to die. When the plant looks dead, your potatoes are ready for digging.
7. Dig down with your hands and uncover the potatoes. They will twist off the vine easily. Shake off the dirt and leave outside to dry for about an hour.
8. Store your potatoes in a cool, dry, dark place until you are ready to eat them.

5.
Have some potato fun

Nobody thinks of the potato as the life of a party (after all, think of the expression "couch potato"). But you can have fun with potatoes. Throw a potato picnic and see for yourself. You can have potato invitations, potato music, potato food (of course) and even some old-fashioned potato games.

Potato sack invitations

You could make invitations on paper with a potato print design. Instructions for potato printing can be found on page 44. Or you could make these one-of-a-kind invites.

For each invitation, you'll need:
   scissors
   light brown paper
   a black marking pen
   a round piece of burlap, about 22 cm (10 inches) across
   a piece of string, ribbon or yarn about 30 cm (12 inches) long

1. Cut a potato shape from the brown paper. Write a message:

A Party!
At Ian's House
on Saturday May 2
at 1:00 p.m.

Don't forget to write the time, the day, and the place.

2. Put the paper potato invitation on the circle of burlap. Bring the edges together until you have a bag. Tie the string around the top with a big bow.

3. Write a message with marker on the front of the bag.

Potato salad

Whenever there's a picnic, you can look forward to two things: ants and potato salad. The potato salad helps make up for those pesky ants. On Prince Edward Island, the potatoes are so popular that people have potato picnics where the games, food and even the dessert have something to do with potatoes. Here is recipe for a perfect potato salad.

You'll need:

6 medium-sized new potatoes
kitchen knife
medium pot
a medium-sized salad bowl
1 hard-boiled egg, cut into small pieces
2 stalks of celery, cut into small pieces
1 green onion, cut into small pieces
125 mL (½ cup) mayonnaise
125 mL (½ cup) plain yogurt or
    sour cream
salt and pepper, if you like

1. Wash and scrub the potatoes but do not peel. Cut each potato into quarters. Boil or steam the potatoes in the pot until they are soft to touch but not mushy.

2. Let the potatoes cool until they are lukewarm. Cut them into cubes and put into the salad bowl.
3. Add all the remaining ingredients and stir gently. Keep your potato salad in the fridge until serving time.
Serves six.

How do you describe an angry potato?
    Boiling mad.

Ever since the potato was first cultivated in South America, artists and songwriters have sung its praises. Here are a few potato song titles you might want to play at your party:
"Mashed Potato Time" was a best-selling record in 1962 for Dee Dee Sharp.
"Ketchup Loves Potatoes" and "Bud the Spud" are Stompin' Tom Connors' favourite tunes.
Louis Armstrong, a famous jazz trumpeter, composed a song called the "Potato Head Blues."

Potato games

A picnic isn't a picnic without games and races. Here are some old stand-bys and some new games.

1. Steal the Potato

Form two teams standing in rows and facing each other about 3 m (10 feet) apart. The first team numbers off. The opposite team numbers off in reverse order, as shown. Put a potato in the centre between the teams. A caller shouts out a number and the players with that number race to pick up the potato. Whoever gets to it first earns a point for her team. When one team reaches the scoring limit you've set, the game is over.

2. Potato Sack Race

Each runner stands inside a potato sack or old pillow case. When the race starts, the runners grip the top of the case and, without letting go, try to be the first to cross the finish line.

Three!

3. Hot Potato

The players sit in a circle. As music plays, the players pass a potato as quickly as possible from one to another. When the music stops, the player holding the hot potato is out. The game continues until everyone has held the hot potato. By the way, *don't* warm up the potato to play the game just in case some one gets burned.

4. Pass the Potato

Divide into teams and stand as shown. The players at the front of each line tuck a potato under their chins then, with their hands behind their backs, pass their potato to the next player in line. If a player touches the potato with his hands or drops it, the potato goes back to the front of the line and the team starts over. The first team to pass the potato to the end of the line wins.

Glossary

Bacteria Microscopic germs. Some cause disease, others cause decay

Calyx The cup-like group of leaves that protect the growing bud and later hold the flower

Cortex The outer layer of cells under the skin of a tuber that stores most of its nutrients

Chlorophyll The chemical inside leaves that gives green plants their colour and is essential for making the plant's food

Chloroplast A plant cell that contains chlorophyll

Dormant Inactive

Elite A seed potato grown in Canada

Eye The part of the potato tuber that contains the buds that sprout into potato plants

Fertilization This occurs when male cells (sperm) in the pollen join with the female cells (ovules) to produce a seed.

Fungicide Chemical that gets rid of fungus

Fungus A plant that has no chlorophyll and feeds off dead or living plants

Gene The part of a cell that stores information about the cell's characteristics to pass on to the next generation

Genetic engineering The process that involves changing the genes of a plant or organism to create something new

Leucoplast The part of a plant that makes starch granules

Meristem The bud of a potato eye from which a potato plant can grow

Nutrients The minerals and vitamins needed for survival. Plants absorb from the ground minerals that have dissolved in water.

Ovary The female part of a flower containing tiny compartments filled with eggs (ovules)

Ovule Tiny egg that develops into a seed after fertilization

Parenchyma cell The part of a plant that makes starch granules

Pesticide Chemical that gets rid of insects

Pistil The female part of the flower. This includes the ovary and ovules.

Pollen A powdery material containing the male sperm that fertilizes the female egg in a plant

Rhizome A thick underground stem that stores starch (and becomes the tuber in the potato plant)

Seed Potato A tuber or part of a tuber with eyes, which is planted to grow potato plants

Sperm The male cell that joins with the female egg to produce a seed

Spore A microscopic cell from a fungus that can reproduce, like the seed of a plant

Stamen The male part of the flower

True Potato Seed The seeds produced in the fruit of the potato plant

Tuber The hard, knobbly part of the potato plant that is known as the potato

Virus A living thing that is smaller than bacteria that lives in a plant and causes disease

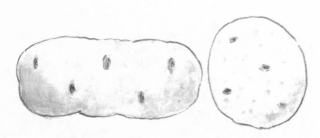

Index

Answers

Check out your chip I.Q., p. 10

1. False. All potato chips are made from raw potatoes.
2. True. Each potato chip is about 6% protein, but that's not as much as in a piece of cheese or a glass of milk.
3. True. Each bag of potato chips gives you more than one-third of the amount of vitamin C that you should have in a day.
4. False. Potato chips are an "extra food." You would have to eat a great deal of them to get the same amount of minerals, vitamins and protein you get from "basic foods" such as pasta, poultry and milk.
5. True and False! You can buy unsalted potato chips, but a small bag of one of the most popular potato chips contains about 500 mg (1/10 teaspoon) of salt — more than you need in a whole day. A small bag of potato chips has almost the same amount of fat as two pats of butter.

The name game, p. 35

Spud — England, Ireland, Scotland; papas — Peru; turma de tierra — West Indies; tartufo — Italy; Kartoffel — Germany; pomme de terre — France; patatas — Philippines, Spain; aardappel — Holland; geo-melon — Greece. The scientific name is *Solanum tuberosum*.

Potato unscramble, p. 42

The words are (clockwise from bottom left): PERU, HARVEST, PEI, CHIP, MASHED, SPROUT, PEEL, STARCH, IDAHO, RUSSET.